Lake District Landscapes

Lake District Landscapes

Dave Coates

MYRIAD BOOKS

First published in 2004 by Myriad Books Limited
35 Bishopsthorpe Road, London SE26 4PA

Photographs and text copyright © Dave Coates

ISBN 1 904154 425

Designed by Jerry Goldie

Printed in China

Contents

Lake District Landscapes

THE LAKE DISTRICT OF CUMBRIA is, without doubt, one of the most beautiful landscapes anyone could wish for, and this is especially true for the photographer. There seems to be a special quality of light that is reserved for this magical corner of England.

In the winter months, with the sun never rising very high in the sky, this clarity of light can last all day and, as a bonus, the dead bracken from the previous summer gives a rich, almost golden colour to the fells. Winter is followed by the freshness of spring and the deep greens of summer, which are complemented, on a fine day, by the deep blue of the sky reflected in the water of the lakes. Even during this time, if you venture out in the early morning or late afternoon and evening, you will find that glorious light for which the Lake District is so renowned. The year is brought to a close with the autumn colours that are at least as spectacular as anywhere else in the British Isles. Those colours can be seen from late September, rising to a crescendo in late October and early November and lasting, in some years, into December. The cycle is then completed by an almost seamless change to winter.

So how, in photographs, does one do justice to this wonderful place, in one book? In the photographer's favour is the fact that the whole of the Lake District is packed into a very small area, barely 30 miles in any direction. Set against this is the fact that so much beauty is crowded into that small space. First of all I have to accept that I shall never be able to cover every corner. What this book does try to do is take you on a photographic journey around the lakes.

Looked at from above it seems that the major lakes tend to flow outwards from the centre like the spokes of some gigantic wheel, with the centre being an axis between the high fells of the Helvellyn and Scafell ranges.

To a certain extent we follow the course of that wheel in an anti-clockwise direction. We start in the north with Bassenthwaite Lake, moving towards the centre and taking in Derwent Water and Borrowdale on the way. We then move out towards the north-west via Buttermere and Crummock Water, before exploring the south-western valleys, including Wasdale. A visit to Coniston, in the south, is followed by a look at the valleys, tarns and lakes of the central Lake District. We then travel south, for a brief look at Windermere and north for Thirlmere, which are followed by

Blencathra and Walla Crag

departing from the centre again, this time towards the north-east and our final lake of Ullswater.

As the journey progresses the book hopes to share with you, through my photographs, the glory that is the Lake District landscape in all its seasons. For me landscape photography is a passion that has enabled me to capture some of those unforgettable moments when the quality of light and the beauty of the countryside come together. It is often said that landscape photography is not so much photographing the land, more photographing the light, as it falls on the land. This was never more true than in the Lake District.

Dave Coates

Chapter 1

Bassenthwaite and around Keswick

IN THIS REGION which contains so much water it seems natural to start our journey with a lake. And there is really only one choice: Bassenthwaite. This is the only "lake" in the Lake District, all the rest being "waters", "meres" or "tarns". Bassenthwaite is at the heart of the Lakes and makes a natural starting point for visitors. At the beginning of the year the sun rises over the lake in spectacular fashion, as shown in the photographs on this and the next page. From Bassenthwaite this photographic journey meanders around the hills and dales that surround the town of Keswick, at the head of the lake, including the ancient stone circle at Castlerigg and the beautiful Newlands Valley.

Bassenthwaite dawn

There could not be a better time to start this journey than at dawn. Bassenthwaite Lake is partly frozen over on a cold December morning and the hills behind have a dusting of snow. There is a cold, grey feel to the day yet in the distance the sky is beginning to glow with the promise of a sunrise to follow.

Dodd Fell sunrise

Bassenthwaite is only 70ft (21m) deep and is fringed with rich vegetation. Once the sun has risen from the south-east over the fell the appearance of the lake changes dramatically. The sky becomes suffused with gorgeous orange and yellow hues while the lake and the mist also take on the same colours. Gradually the day begins to warm up.

The softer colours of sunrise

As the sun rises higher in the sky the colours begin to soften a little and shades of blue in the sky begin to mingle with the pink. Even when the sun disappears behind a passing cloud there is still enough bright light in the sky to begin to drive away the colours of dawn.

Pre dawn glow across the lake

On a cloudy morning the dawn light can still be attractive, although the colours are often subtle and subdued. Here, a tree growing out of the water is silhouetted against patches of sunlight on the lake.

The moment of sunrise

In this photograph the sun has just risen and its first light plays dramatically across the surface of the lake. The patches of ice and the frosted remains of last year's reeds grouped around the shoreline are the first objects which catch the rays of the rising sun. The clear light of dawn lasts for only a very short time before the sun fully clears the fells and climbs into the sky.

Skiddaw on a winter's afternoon

One of the great fells near Keswick is Skiddaw, which stands at over 3,000ft (915m)
and dominates the countryside around it. Seen here on a winter's afternoon, the soft
watery sunlight plays on the landscape as the sheep forage in the foreground.

Blencathra and St John's in the Vale

The hills around the Keswick area are striking, and none more so than the distinctive shape of Blencathra (2,847ft/868m), which is seen here as a snow-covered backdrop to this view down St John's in the Vale. This photograph is taken from a spot near Thirlmere.

Blencathra in snow

The dramatic skyline of Blencathra is shown to good effect with the morning light bringing out the very best in this snow-clad landscape. In the foreground is an old section, now largely unused, of the A66 which leads to the heart of the northern lakes.

Autumn mists in the valley

Before the sun has risen high enough to reach over the surrounding fells and into the bottom of Newlands Valley, the mists on this September day combine with an early frost to give a quiet but wonderfully peaceful feel to the scene.

Looking up Newlands towards Knott Rigg

Newlands Valley is surrounded by the north-western fells and Knott Rigg in particular dominates this scene. In the late summer sunshine, we look up the valley towards Newlands Pass which carries the motorist out of the top of the valley and then down again into Buttermere village.

May blossom in Newlands Valley

To the west of Keswick is Newlands Valley, shown here in the spring. No lakes here, just a lovely valley surrounded by the high fells. Cattle graze in the fields, while the May blossom in its full glory adds to the beauty of the landscape. The fell of Hindscarth rises up in the distance to create a perfect backdrop to this scene.

Newlands Valley

It was a dull and cold wind-blown November day when this photograph was taken. For some time there had been total cloud cover. Then suddenly, as often happens in the Lakes, alternate cloud and sunshine swept repeatedly over the same patch of landscape. This photograph, which is so enhanced by the dramatic effect of sunlight, was well worth the wait.

Autumn colours (left)
This little scene, taken quite close to the woodland path, above, on the shores of Bassenthwaite, seems to say such a lot about autumn in a Lakeland wood. The golden colours of the bracken and birch tree contrast sharply with the green of the conifers behind.

Woodland path near Bassenthwaite
This photograph is taken on a dull day with barely any sunlight on a woodland path between Keswick and Bassenthwaite at the foot of Skiddaw and Great Dodd. The colours are soft and rich and the absence of strong light means there are no harsh shadows.

Castlerigg stone circle in storm light

To the east of Keswick on a raised shoulder of land, but surrounded on all sides by the high fells of the northern lakes, lies the ancient stone circle of Castlerigg. In one of the most dramatic settings imaginable for such a monument, storm clouds can be seen in the distance over the Helvellyn range contrasting with the sunlight on the stones.

Standing stone

In the winter afternoon's light this single stone stands out against the landscape. You can almost feel the texture of the stone thanks to the interplay of the light and shade caused by a mixture of clouds and clear sky.

Summer morning at Castlerigg

The stone circle dates from about 2000BC and consists of 38 stones in the circle and 10 at its centre. It is formed from volcanic Borrowdale rock which was swept through the region by Ice Age glaciers. Looking at this photograph, it is easy to let your imagination run: the larger stone could almost be a high priest standing in front of his flock who are kneeling in prayer before him. On this early morning in July, the sun has cast a soft but glowing light on the stones which only seems to add to the air of mystery that surrounds the scene.

Single stone and Skiddaw

The enigmatic shapes of the individual stones of the Castlerigg stone circle can take on a "sculptural" quality, especially when the sun is low in the sky. This stone, set against Skiddaw in the late afternoon sun, is a good example.

The stones reflected (right)

It was a cold February morning and recent rain had left a pool of water in the centre of the stone circle. Low winter sun came from behind a cloud to illuminate the view. The summit of Blencathra, which looks over Castlerigg from the north-east, is reflected in the pool as the warm light almost brings the stones to life.

Looking towards Helvellyn in the snow

A touch of snow makes a dramatic difference to the scene. Photographed on a winter's afternoon, this view towards the Dodds and Helvellyn range has an altogether different atmosphere once snow has fallen.

Winter – Skiddaw from the head of the lake

This is a typical picture of Derwent Water in the winter. On a clear day the winter colours of the reeds in the foreground contrast with the blue of the sky. This photograph was taken from the duckboards which carry the footpath across the vulnerable marshlands at the head of the lake. In the foreground there are icy pools with frosted grasses and reeds; in the distance are the peaks of Skiddaw and Walla Crag (1,243ft/379m).

Chapter 2

Derwent Water and Borrowdale

THE NORTH-EASTERN shore of Derwent Water lies at the very edge of Keswick and is directly upstream of Bassenthwaite Lake. Located beneath the fells of Cat Bells and Skiddaw it is one of the larger of the Lake District's lakes and at its widest point is 1¼ miles (2.8km) across. The journey continues towards the high fells with a visit to the valley of Borrowdale. The unique landscape of Borrowdale was formed by glacial action which resulted in a steep moraine gorge and a flood plain overlooked by dramatic fell scenery on all sides.

Spring – Manesty Woods and Walla Crag

This photograph is taken at the south-western corner of Derwent Water near Manesty. The flowering gorse and fresh leaves on the trees tell us that spring has arrived with all the promise of summer to come. A still day adds to the mood with the mirror-like reflection of a welcoming blue sky and soft white clouds. Blencathra and Walla Crag take on a blueish hue as they stand in shadow in the background.

Summer – Derwent Water and the Jaws of Borrowdale

This photograph was taken on a fine summer's morning overlooking Derwent Water from Falcon Crag. There are glorious views in every direction at this location. The dazzling sky and still lake contribute to a feeling of peace as we look across to the Jaws of Borrowdale on the left and the fells of High Spy and Maiden Head on the far side.

Autumn – Blencathra from Manesty

Seen from the fells above Manesty, shortly after sunrise, Derwent Water is shrouded in autumn mists that seem to flow across the lake and cling to the flanks of Skiddaw and Blencathra. The gorse bushes, some still flowering well into autumn, seem to enhance the autumn colour of the trees below.

Manesty Woods autumn mists

Overlooking the lake the autumn colours of the bracken and the trees are enhanced by the traces of mist which drift up from the lake beyond. The early morning light streaming towards the camera has the effect of creating almost incandescent colours in the trees.

Manesty winter's day (right)

The stark contrast between the frosted grasses in the foreground and the darker colours of the trees on the far side of the lake makes this scene come to life. The reflection of the sunlit trees in the still water at the corner of Derwent Water seems to heighten that contrast.

Derwent Water storm clouds

The wind was quite strong on a stormy day with the clouds scudding across the sky creating ever changing moods when this photograph was taken. Looking north down the lake towards Skiddaw, the strong south-westerly wind broke up the clouds giving short bursts of sunlight.

Frosty morning at the head of Derwent Water

The photographs above and right were taken on a cold morning at the head of Derwent Water near Manesty. Here we look back along the duckboards which stretch across the marshes towards Lodore. The sun shining down from the fell lit up the frosted grasses, the trees and the sweep of the footway. All of these contrasted with the fell, which is in deep shadow.

Headwaters of the lake

The sun has just risen on the eastern side of the lake leaving the fells in deep shadow but casting its spell over the distant trees and the water itself. From this quiet spot, it is difficult to appreciate that Derwent Water opens out into a great expanse of water – the widest of all the lakes in the Lake District.

Manesty tree view

At this spot close to the headwaters of the lake we look directly towards the fells. The effect of the low winter sun highlights the contrast between the sunlit flood plain and the darkness of the fells in shadow behind. The touch of snow on the fells and the richness of the dead grasses simply add to the atmosphere.

Autumn light in Great Wood

The Great Wood below Walla Crag is a beautiful stretch of woodland. The foresters who added the conifers to the natural woodland of Great Wood left us with this line of tree trunks which seem to contrast starkly with the many different leaves of nearby deciduous trees. The power of the light streaming down through the leaves and branches, coupled with the use of a soft-focus filter, helps to create this typical image of this well-known wood.

Ashness Bridge

Ashness Bridge, on an ancient packhorse route, is a popular location for visitors to Derwent Water. The classic views of the stream and the bridge, coupled with the distant view of Derwent Water and Skiddaw, demonstrate why it is one of the Lake District's most popular spots. On a cold March day, the cloud cover gives only short breaks of sunlight. Waiting for the right combination of light and shadow can be time-consuming, but the ever-changing patterns of light are always captivating.

Blencathra and Walla Crag

All three of the landscapes on these pages were taken within a few feet of each other on a glorious autumn morning, from the roadway on the western side of the lake which overlooks the lake near Manesty Woods. This first photograph shows the overall view out and across the lake towards Blencathra and Walla Crag and catches the autumn colours in the bracken and the trees against a picturesque blue sky and lake.

Manesty Woods

This view looks down the fell into Manesty Woods below. The morning light illuminates this scene with the trees in their autumn colours surrounding the little green clearing in the woods.

Birch trees on the crags

The glorious sight of the birch trees in their very best autumn colours is caught in this photograph looking up the fell face with the trees set against the sky. The fact that the trees manage to survive, let alone prosper, in such a rocky environment is impressive.

Ferry tied up in evening light

As one of the larger lakes, Derwent Water enjoys a scheduled ferry service to various points around the lake from the boat landings at Keswick. The late afternoon light has enhanced the colours of this scene with the ferry tied up at the Keswick boat landings. Both Skiddaw behind and the reflections in the water seem to glow in the warmth of the light.

Sunset over Derwent Water

The boat landings at Derwent Water have always attracted photographers seeking a lakeland sunset. On this November day ducks drift peacefully in the foreground while the last rays of sunlight burst in dramatic fashion from behind Causey Pike (2,089ft/637m). The lake itself glows with the reflection of the golden colours of the sunset.

Ferry approaching the landings in winter light

This photograph was taken around lunchtime on what was an otherwise grey November day. Suddenly, a small break in the clouds appeared giving dramatic shafts of light across the lake creating a magical, almost monochromatic scene, as the ferry came in toward the boat landings.

Grange Bridge in Borrowdale

Situated snuggly in the bottom of the Borrowdale Gorge is the lovely village of Grange. The narrow but beautiful old bridge that gives access to the village from the main valley road is seen here basking in the midday sun, with the rugged sunlit fells behind only serving to emphasise the gorge-like nature of the location.

River Derwent towards Cockley Howe

The River Derwent, which feeds into Derwent Water, flows down the rocky moraine gorge of Borrowdale. There is an ever-changing scene with trees clinging to the banks as the fells rise upwards from the course of the river. In this picture, looking down river towards Cockley Howe, the steep sides of the valley create an impressive backdrop with the bracken reflected in the water.

Rosthwaite from Eelstep Brow

This photograph of the flood plain area of Borrowdale was taken around midday in January and from the same place as the gorge photographs below and opposite. With the light streaming towards the camera the mood is totally different as the residents of the hamlet of Rosthwaite stoke up their fires for Sunday lunch.

Borrowdale from Eelstep Brow

Looking down Borrowdale, the sides of the gorge are in deep shadow
due to the low winter sun but the foreground rocks and the tree
provide a strong foil. The snow-clad fell tops, against a clear blue sky,
almost resemble the icing on a cake.

Across the gorge from Eelstep Brow

Eelstep Brow in Borrowdale is much-loved by visitors. A short walk
up the fell from the road below, it presents you with dramatic vistas
in all directions. This atmospheric view of the trees across the gorge
and the slopes of Maiden Head beyond was taken on the same
January day and at about the same time.

Spring light in a disused slate quarry

The trees in Borrowdale are beautiful whatever the season or weather conditions. Here the fresh silver birch leaves of spring glow against the grey debris of this disused quarry. The morning sun seems to spotlight them helped by the light bouncing off the surrounding slabs of slate.

Borrowdale standing stone

In this area you will come across a number of standing stones – including the famous Bowder stone – deposited by Ice Age glaciers. The standing stone at the head of the gorge, pictured here, may have arrived naturally – although it looks as though it has been placed here by human hand, rather like the famous Castlerigg stone circle.

Sycamore tree in the rain

On a rainy day in autumn, this sycamore tree, with its golden foliage, stands out from the background. Beyond, the soft colours of the other trees and the more subtle hues of the fell provide an interesting contrast.

Looking into Borrowdale from Honister

Taken early one morning from part-way down the pass and looking into Borrowdale, this photograph shows shafts of early morning light highlighting the mist in the valley bottom below. It is easy to see why some people claim that Borrowdale is the loveliest valley in England.

Light and shadows from Honister Pass

The road through Borrowdale eventually climbs out of the valley towards Buttermere via the infamous Honister Pass with its steep road and reputation for rapid changes in the weather. This view looks back down and across Borrowdale from near the top of the pass. It was taken on a day of changing light with the sun highlighting parts of the landscape.

Chapter 3

Buttermere and Crummock Water

AT THE HEAD of Borrowdale our journey follows the main road that makes its dramatic climb out of the valley via Honister Pass and down into the Buttermere valley. This valley is closely surrounded by some of the most famous of the lakeland fells, such as Fleetwith Pike, Haystacks, Red Pike and Robinson. On a still day the lake acts like a mirror and the way the light plays into the valley from between the fell tops creates spectacular lighting conditions, adding to the beauty of this place. Crummock Water is the next lake downstream from Buttermere; less well-known than its illustrious neighbours, it is a wonderful place to linger – and an ideal spot to get away from the crowds.

Winter – the ash tree

As the winter sun passes between the fells of Brandreth and Haystacks it illuminates this lone tree standing on a promontory of land beside Buttermere; the fell on the far side is in shadow, creating an almost surreal effect.

Spring – Haystacks and the lake

The gorse bushes coming into flower signal the regeneration of spring and also form a natural foreground to this picture. It was taken in the early stillness of a May morning looking across the head of the lake and on towards Haystacks. At 1,732ft (528m) it was one of the favourite peaks of Alfred Wainwright, the author of the classic guides to walking in the Lakes.

Summer – the isolated tree

Trees are particularly important in landscape photography. Here, on a glorious August morning, we look up Buttermere with High Crag on the right. This isolated and waterbound tree adds interest to an otherwise plain but summery sky.

Autumn – the Char Hut and Gatesgarth

As autumn advances, the grasses fade and the bracken turns a rich golden brown. Looking across the head of the lake towards Gatesgarth Farm and Honister Pass, the autumn colours and the old char hut are reflected in the almost still water. The hut is used as a place for fishermen to store their gear and gets its name from the char – a fish which is a close relative of the trout or salmon, but much smaller in size.

Dubbs Quarry

It is easy to forget that the Lake District had an industrial past but here, high on the flanks of Fleetwith Pike (2,126ft/648m), which overlooks Buttermere, are the remains of a slate quarry. With a wonderful feel for the environment, one of the old ruined buildings has been tastefully renovated and turned into a mountain refuge hut. The tension between this and the ruins to the left add a touch of poignancy to the scene.

Buttermere and Crummock Water from the descent path

Fleetwith Pike is located at the southern end of Buttermere. The return path from its flanks leads the fell-walker back to Gatesgarth Farm and offers this wonderful view of Buttermere with Crummock Water in the distance. The late afternoon light on this glorious summer's day only serves to bring the lakes and the surrounding hills to life.

Innominate Tarn and Pillar with heather

It is said that Innominate Tarn –
so-called because it has no name
– seen here in the middle
distance with Pillar as a
backdrop, was one of the
favourite places of the late
Alfred Wainwright. Indeed,
Wainwright loved the place so
much that he arranged to have
his ashes strewn around
Haystacks, close to the Tarn.
It certainly is an atmospheric
spot – wander through the rocky
hummocks and a different view
opens up at every turn.

The Buttermere pines

One can often capture the essence of a whole scene by carefully selecting a small section of it. This view of the Buttermere Pines – a line of trees stretching along the shore of Buttermere – illustrates the point well. The early morning sun lights up the trees but leaves the fells behind in an almost indistinct haze, so enhancing its effect on the trees.

Buttermere reflections in early autumn

The sight of Buttermere on a fine morning is breathtaking. The reflections from the steep fellsides are so real that you feel that you could almost step into them. The light and shadows cast by the low sun as it rises between the peaks creates a sight that is truly magnificent. Buttermere was once voted the second most beautiful place in England. But for many people, it is their favourite beauty spot.

Sunlit trees

To photographers the beauty of the row of Scots pines at the head of the lake is well-known. Here the early morning sun, having risen above Robinson (2,417ft/737m), illuminates the trees giving them an almost incandescent quality while the mass of Fleetwith Pike casts a contrasting shadow on the fells behind.

Fleetwith Pike and Haystacks

On this misty October morning, the silhouettes of Fleetwith Pike on the left and Haystacks on the right play an almost secondary role to the glory of the light in the sky and the mists that are swirling across Buttermere. The warmth of the early sun adds a touch of colour to the mists which seem to almost reach up to the top of the fells.

The not so lone tree

This is another view of the trees along the shore of Buttermere. Again the fall of the light is important as it leaves the slope of High Style in the background in shadow. The unusual shape of the birches in the foreground provides a frame for the lone ash tree in the distance. For once, the absence of reflections in the water is a bonus.

Rannerdale Knotts and the peninsula

The surface of Crummock Water had almost stilled when this photograph was taken at about noon on a lovely late September day. The little peninsula of land that reaches out into the lake leads across to the rocky hummocks of Rannerdale Knotts and Whiteless Pike in the centre background.

Loweswater Fell

Loweswater Fell is one of the quietest and least visited corners of the Lake District. This photograph was taken on an autumn day when light was at a premium and the landscape was an ever-changing pattern of colour and shadow. Everything seemed to come together here, with the variety of colours on the scree balanced by the sheep grazing peacefully below. The solitary tree seems to emphasise the feeling of wilderness.

A little birch tree on the side of Melbreak

The blackness of the heather high on the side of Melbreak Fell acts as a perfect foil to the lonely little silver birch tree.
The spring sunshine highlights its fresh young leaves and the distinctive bark of its trunk as it stands in splendid
isolation. At 1,688ft (514m) Melbreak rises suddenly and steeply on Crummock Water's western shore.

The last light of autumn (left)

One can often walk the fells on a dull day in the hope that at some point the sun will poke through the clouds just long enough for you to take a picture. It was such a day one November when we were walking on the fells alongside Langthwaite Green near Crummock Water. With the leaves almost gone from the trees this photograph could easily be named "the last light of autumn".

The thorn tree, looking toward Grasmoor and Whiteless Pike

The prevailing winds can bend exposed trees into some interesting shapes and this thorn tree on the fellside overlooking Crummock Water is a good example. The photograph was taken with the camera near to the ground so that it framed the view across the lake to the mass of Grasmoor. The little patch of cloud is a piece of good luck which helps complete the picture.

Chapter 4

Wasdale, Eskdale and Duddon Valley

FROM THE north-western lakes and valleys we now move south to explore the south-western valleys. We start with Wasdale, which has its own brand of dramatic scenery, reaching as it does to the foot of some of the high fells including Scafell, the highest mountain in England. We then move over the fells to Eskdale before crossing the Hardknott Pass to take a look at the Duddon Valley. Surrounded by wild fells, these two valleys do not contain any lakes but make up for this with their dramatic and breathtaking scenery.

Winter's light, Wastwater

As the nights shorten and the sun comes round into the south-west in the afternoon, Wastwater and its magnificent, if slightly forbidding scree slopes, can be seen at their very best. On a February afternoon with the wind blowing lazily but icily down the lake, the sun suddenly bursts from under an almost unbroken layer of cloud to provide this wonderfully lit view of Wastwater and its threatening slopes.

Yewbarrow landscape

This photograph was taken on a trip to Wasdale in the hope of catching the light on the lake. On a dull winter's day there was just a hope that the light might break through the clouds. We were in luck – driving up the dale the light did break through lighting up the snow-capped summit of Yewbarrow (1,985ft/600m) together with the field and trees next to the road. Yewbarrow is not a high peak in comparison to many in the Lakes but its wonderful shape and steep crags are an inspiring sight.

The last light on the screes

For a photographer there is little to match the effects of the sunlight on the screes. This view was taken as the sun was going down over the horizon, resulting in the vivid detail and relief in the screes and the intense colours of the reflections. The sun was so low in the sky that barely seconds later the gravel in the foreground fell into shadow.

Yewbarrow and Wastwater with storm clouds

Wasdale has many moods and they can change quite dramatically. On this day the mixture of cloud and light created this powerful scene. With only dappled sunlight on Yewbarrow and Great Gable (2,924ft/891m) behind, the clouds take on a dynamic and almost threatening mood and yet there is still a welcoming warmth in the landscape.

Sheep in the fields

A few minutes before taking the photograph of Yewbarrow (above) this group of sheep appeared. They were lazing contentedly in the autumn sunshine in a field barely a few hundred yards from the lake. The back lighting has rim-lit the sheep and enriched the colours in the leaves of the old oak tree under which they graze.

Lakeside boathouse

Wander around the shores of the lake and you will come across this little boathouse at the water's edge. The light this October day came and went in short, erratic bursts. The craggy fells of Whin Rigg, which guard the far side of the lake, tower over the scene giving a sense of scale to the landscape.

The Upper Eskdale Valley

Park near the foot of Hardknott Pass and wander into the beautiful valley that is Upper Eskdale. The only sounds are of the wind and the water as it passes over numerous waterfalls. Although well-known as the starting point for hikers exploring the Scafell range, the less energetic can still enjoy the beauty of this peaceful dale surrounded by views of some of the grandest mountains of the Lake District.

Esk Falls, Eskdale

The Esk Falls, which carry the infant river on its journey down from Great Moss, are located just above Lincove Bridge. They are just one of a brace of sparkling waterfalls to be found at this location where the river passes through a narrow gorge.

Eskdale waterfall

As you make your way up the valley you will find
the watercourse almost littered with waterfalls.
This is just one of many examples; it has no name
but typifies the way the River Esk tumbles its way
down the dale. If you look into the water as you
walk, especially in the rock pools, you will find
that it takes on deep, almost unreal but beautiful shades
of blue and green.

Duddon Valley Fells
(right)
On the left of the photograph is the shadowy form of Harter Fell. At 2,139ft (652m) it is one of the higher peaks of the central lakeland and dominates this view of Duddon Valley with the high fells of the Lake District in the distance. The rough, craggy and rock-strewn nature of Duddon Valley is clearly seen in this photograph taken from the road which leads over Kiln Bank and the Dunnerdale Fells.

Tarn Beck and the Seathwaite Fells
A popular walk in Duddon Valley takes you up the line of Tarn Beck and then onto the Seathwaite Fells. As you wander down from the parking area by the main road you come to a little footbridge which takes you over the beck. On the left is the view of the route ahead from the footbridge. There is a real feeling of wilderness about this landscape, despite its proximity to the road. Once onto the fells you find yourself in a geat bowl in the hills and ahead of you is the wall of fell (right) that separates Duddon Valley from Coniston. The fell includes a number of well-known points of interest including the peaks of Swirl How (2,637ft/804m) and the Old Man of Coniston (2,364ft/803m). At your feet is Seathwaite Tarn. The tarn is about 800m in length and any surplus water is carried from it down Tarn Beck into Duddon Valley.

Chapter 5
Coniston and Tarn Hows

FROM DUDDON VALLEY we move over the range of fells dominated by the Old Man of Coniston to Coniston Water itself and to Tarn Hows, which lies nearby. The small town of Coniston – "king's village" – lies at the head of the lake and under the lea of the Old Man of Coniston, whose lower slopes provided work for the town's inhabitants in its industrial past. The beautifully located waters of Tarn Hows were once actually three smaller tarns until, in the 19th century, their enterprising owner dammed the outflow and made them into the larger, but more splendid, single tarn that we see today.

Coniston Water with Coniston town and the Old Man

The Old Man of Coniston towers majestically above Coniston Water and the little town that gives its name to the lake. The Old Man provides a grand backdrop to almost any view of the lake and on this fine day, with the blue sky so boldly reflected in the lake below, its snow-covered summit only serves to add to the spectacle. The restored Victorian steam yacht *Gondola* sails from Coniston pier to jetties around the lake.

Coniston Town under the lea of the Old Man

Look more closely at those hills which seem to crowd over the homesteads of Coniston and you will realise that town and fell are deeply entwined in their industrial past. The waterfall that tumbles down the fell carrying Levers Water Beck towards the town flows past numerous old spoil heaps left over from times past when the copper mining industry held sway.

Levers Water Beck

The river which flows out of Levers Water looks as cold and grey as the weather in this photograph. Even the rocks over which the water flows have a cold and unwelcoming look to them. A slow shutter speed coupled with the use of a tripod has helped capture this atmospheric scene.

Levers Water

Fifteen hundred feet (457m) high in the fells that overlook Coniston, and in a bowl hidden from the valley below, is Levers Water, a reservoir hugged by the steep-sided fells of Little and Great How, Raven Tor and High Fell. This picture, taken on a cold grey March day when photography looked out of the question, shows the still grey coldness of the water and the beauty of a desolate landscape.

Coniston Water on a misty day

There are many days when the high peaks around Coniston seem to encourage a haze to settle over the narrow lake. And yet despite the mist, the natural beauty of the surroundings shines through and atmospheric images of the water and mountains appear in every direction.

Tarn Hows with Weatherlam

Tarn Hows, a collection of three tarns now merged into one, lies on the lower fells to the north of Coniston and must be one of the most visited of all the tarns in the Lakes. Beatrix Potter purchased the site as part of an estate and donated it to the National Trust. On this fine November morning, with the colours of autumn in the trees, the still water reflects the sky like a mirror. Weatherlam (2,500ft/762m) stands high in the background overlooking the tree-lined tarn.

Tarn in autumn

This little tarn, surrounded by trees in their autumn colours, is very evocative of early winter in the Lake District. Beautiful reflections can be seen in the clear, still waters at the edge of the tarn.

Tree at Tarn Hows

This photograph across Tarn Hows displays the variety of trees to be found in the Lakes. The contrast between the old deciduous trees in the foreground, the Scots pines on the little promontory and the golden conifers behind illustrates this.

Tarn Hows with the Langdale Pikes

If you climb up the slopes surrounding Tarn Hows you are rewarded by spectacular views across the Lake District fells. The familiar peaks of the Langdale Pikes, famous among the climbing fraternity, contrast with the tarn and tree-covered fells in the foreground.

Tarn Hows shoreline

There are many beautful scenes to be found on the shores of Tarn Hows. This little stand of silver birch trees in their autumn colours are vividly reflected in the still waters of the tarn and seem to stand out among the greenery surrounding them.

Across the trees into Great Langdale

Great Langdale is one of the most spectacular valleys in the Lakes. This stunning landscape is a paradise for walkers and nature-lovers. Here the snow-dusted fells of Great Langdale seem to glow in the late afternoon light.

Chapter 6

The Langdales

THE LANGDALE VALLEYS lie just to the north of Tarn Hows and are in the very heart of the Lake District. The first valley, Little Langdale, is more popularly known for the narrow and tortuously winding route that takes the traveller from Ambleside to the dramatic Wrynose and Hardknott Passes and over to the western side of the Lake District. Get away from the road and you will find it is indeed one of the many lovely corners to be explored on foot. Near the head of the valley and before you climb to Wrynose Pass, turn right and to the north and you will climb on to the hause (a narrow neck of land) between Little Langdale and its more famous neighbour, Great Langdale. This area is rich in tarns, such as Little Langdale Tarn and Loughrigg Tarn, and is dominated by the Langdale Pikes themselves.

Little Langdale Tarn

Little Langdale Tarn is set in a bowl of land surrounded by an arc of fells. Seen here with Blake Rigg in the distance, this is always an oasis of peace. The natural lie of the land hides the narrow winding road that leads through the dale. You would be hard-pressed to pick out the road if it were not for the cottages at Fell Foot and Busk House. In fact the road enters at Wrynose Pass on the left, comes down into the valley bottom across the picture and then leaves on the right.

Slater's Bridge

Barely a few hundred yards downstream from the tarn is Slater's Bridge. Set in a glorious landscape with its lovely arch of local stone, this little bridge is a fine example of an old lakeland packhorse bridge. It must be one of the finest treasures of the Lake District; sadly, it has been necessary for safety reasons to instal a black metal handrail over its graceful form.

Greenburn Reservoir with Swirl How and Hell Gill Pike

Follow the route of Greenburn Beck up into the fells from Little Langdale Tarn and you will eventually come to Greenburn Reservoir. Originally built to support mine-workings, the small sheet of water sits beneath Weatherlam. In the distance the line of fells sweeps from Swirl How on the left round past Hell Gill Pike (2,172ft/662m) in the centre to the euphemistically named Wet Side Edge.

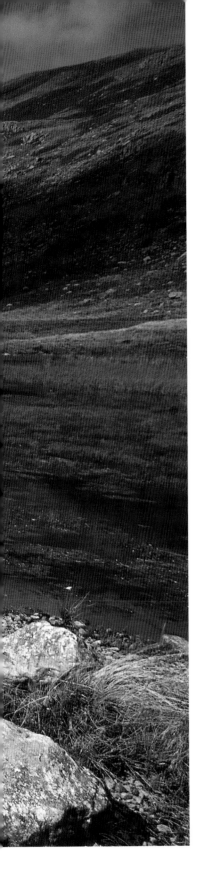

Little Langdale from Greenburn mine workings

The view from the old mine-workings at Greenburn is breathtaking. Looking east with Little Langdale Tarn below the view extends past Loughrigg Fell in the middle distance to the fells of Scandale and the Red Screes.

Un-named tarn on Greenburn Moor

This little pool of water, with its cotton grasses and contrasting patch of red vegetation, is typical of the landscape of the Lakeland fells. A glorious summer sky completes the scene.

Frozen tarn and the Langdale Pikes

Blea Tarn lies in the hause between the valleys of Great and Little Langdale. Here the frozen tarn with its lovely soft reflection is set against the backdrop of Side Pike at the far end of the tarn. The icy foreground and the golden grasses on the far shore glow in the winter sunshine, with the sombre form of the distant Langdale Pikes as a backdrop.

Langdale Pikes

The fall of the light on the fells was never as important as in this photograph of the Langdale Pikes, taken near Blea Tarn. Every shadow plays its part in emphasising the graphic form and grandeur of the Pikes as they tower above the valleys hidden below.

Trees and frost patterns

This image captures perfectly the mood of Blea Tarn on a cold winter's day. The mixture of bare conifers, and the Scots pines beyond, stand in contrast to the sheet of ice on the tarn.

Lingmoor Fell and Tarn

Lingmoor Fell separates the valleys of Great and Little Langdale. It is not a particularly high fell nor is it visually impressive from a distance, but almost hidden in its hummock-covered summit is Lingmoor Tarn, a sleepy stretch of water which provides a green oasis surrounded by the contrasting heather-clad fells. With its lovely irregular shape, set among the crags, the tarn almost appears to defy gravity as it seems to hang precariously over the edge of the fell overlooking Great Langdale. Once away from the high fells and down at the water's edge you appreciate the intimate nature of this tarn.

Heather and stone with the Langdale Pikes

The heather on Lingmoor Fell acts as a colourful foreground and counterbalance to this view of the Langdale Pikes.
In the distant shadows is the tumbling watercourse of Stickle Ghyll. The Pikes, a cluster of shapely hilltops, radiate
out from Harrison Stickle at their centre. They provide some of the most dramatic ascents in the Lakes.

Rowan tree and heather

The rowan tree, or mountain ash, is to be found throughout the Lakeland fells. The rowan is at its best in late summer when its bright red berries are on display. This little tree grows out of a rocky hillock on Lingmoor Fell. It is typical of the way that these sturdy trees compete for the available space between the rocks.

Blea Tarn and the Tilberthwaite Fells

This is one of the many views to be enjoyed from Lingmoor Fell, and includes Blea Tarn which is overlooked by Blake Rigg on the right. In the distance is the looming bulk of Weatherlam. The Tarn and the valley bottom is bathed in beautiful late afternoon sunlight, which also picks out the heather in the foreground

Great Langdale with Pike of Stickle

Known and loved by generations of fell-walkers, Great Langdale is a glacial valley which, from the evidence of the flood plain in this photograph, contained a sizeable lake in years gone by. Now the great fells tower above the green fields in which the Herdwick sheep, the traditional breed of the lakes, graze so peacefully. Bow Fell (2,959ft/902m), capped in snow, is seen on the left appearing over the flanks of the Langdale Pikes with Pike of Stickle (2,324/723m) showing on the right of the skyline.

View from High Close across to Weatherlam

Taken with a telephoto lens, this photograph across the ridge between Great and Little Langdale to the fell of Weatherlam in the distance captures the drama that can be found when the sun breaks through the clouds on an otherwise dull afternoon. The effect of the light on the clouds and surrounding landscape is striking.

Harrison Stickle

On a clear January day the highest of the Langdale Pikes, Harrison Stickle (2,415ft /736m) stands out well against the blue sky above. The waters of Stickle Ghyll can be seen crashing down the gully as they make their way from Stickle Tarn into Great Langdale below.

Raven Crag from High Close

Raven Crag (1,520ft/461m) in Great Langdale, is a summit which attracts many visitors and walkers. With the sun low in the sky and the valley bottom in deep shadow, the Crag appears to stand out even more powerfully. The hillside comes to life and the trees below are almost on fire with the vibrant colours of autumn.

Elterwater Village and the Langdale Pikes

The lovely village of Elterwater, located towards the lower part of Great Langdale, is seen here photographed from its adjoining open common land. Basking in the autumn sun, with seasonal colours all around it, the village lies beneath the shadow of Lingmoor Fell on the left and the familiar shape of the Langdale Pikes beyond.

Elterwater in late autumn light

Elterwater itself lies just down valley from the village of the same name. This photograph is taken in late afternoon in mid November from High Close on the road that leads over from Grasmere. The autumn colours were at their very best and the low light streaming through the trees towards the camera lens captures the enchantment of autumn in the lakes.

Loughrigg Tarn on a late spring morning

At the foot of Great Langdale and tucked away under the lea of Loughrigg Fell is another of the little tarns that adorn this part of the Lake District. On a glorious May morning the water in the tarn is still and reflects Loughrigg Fell behind like a mirror. The fresh spring foliage of the trees surrounding the tarn is enhanced by the clarity and strength of the early morning sunlight.

Tarn-side view in late spring

The morning sunshine catches the spring flowers and the leaves of the water lily plants as they float on the surface of the water at the side of Loughrigg Tarn. The stillness of the water and the overall feeling of tranquillity makes this a spot where you would like to linger for a while.

Loughrigg Tarn and Fell

If you visit Loughrigg Tarn in winter, this place of quiet beauty takes on a different mood compared with other times of the year. Looking out over the still and partly frozen water to Loughrigg Fell the landscape, which is framed by the shrubbery and bullrushes in the foreground, is suffused with rich winter colours.

Loughrigg Tarn – the gnarled tree

This tree (above and below) with its gnarled roots is on the shores of Loughrigg Tarn and has been photographed many times. On the the the morning that the photograph above was taken, the sun was starting to break up the ice on the tarn, and the air reverberated with booming, almost eerie cracks. The photograph below is of the same tree but this time taken from the other side.

Chapter 7
Grasmere and Rydal Water

LOUGHRIGG FELL separates Loughrigg Tarn and the popular and beautiful twin lakes of Grasmere and Rydal Water. These two lakes, which are steeped in the culture and history of the Lake District, have their own intimate qualities for the landscape photographer. While both are small enough to wander around in a single day, between them they have so many attractions that there is rarely enough time to explore them and the surrounding area.

Grasmere from Loughrigg Terrace

Grasmere is seen here from the slopes of Loughrigg Terrace, which has extensive views along the whole of its length. Looking northward to the village of Grasmere just beyond the lake, the gap in the skyline is Dunmail Raise, which the main road passes over on its way to Thirlmere. The gravel "beach" which you can see at the foot of the lake is a favourite with visitors for paddling and for picnics.

Grasmere and the Lion and the Lamb

On a day of changing light with sun and shadows moving across the fells, this photograph of Grasmere shows the evocatively-named Lion and Lamb Fell in shadow, with the fells of Far Easdale catching the sunlight. The whole effect is enhanced by the band of sunshine which gives a lift to the area around the lake and highlights the homesteads along the shore.

Wyke Cottage

The slopes surrounding Grasmere are scattered with many lovely cottages, built in traditional lakeland stone and slate. Wyke Cottage, seen here in June with its lovely garden in full colour, is a fine example. The haphazard design of the house and its wonderful circular chimneys only serve to add to its rustic beauty..

93

Rydal Water southside

With all the summer walkers and picnickers gone, the lakeside walk around Rydal Water takes on a wonderfully peaceful mood. For those who venture out there is the reward of the dramatic winter colours, which are so evident in this photograph of one of the Lake District's most popular beauty spots.

Rydal Water with frost

Rydal Water lies just round the corner from Grasmere with the outflow from Grasmere feeding into it. On a cold but beautiful winter's morning the water's edge is covered in ice. Stripped of their leaves, the stand of trees on the peninsula is reflected clearly in the still smooth waters of the lake.

Winter colours on Rydal

In the late afternoon the watery sun is just about to dip below the fells but is still strong enough to light up the little island and the trees on the left. The soft muted colours of the background fells have already fallen into shadow.

Path through the trees

These woods have a network of footpaths, which lead through this enchanting wonderland of autumn colours. Even on this dull day the colours of the leaves glow with the dark, more severe shapes of the tree trunks adding an element of stark contrast. The woodland floor is clothed in a carpet of bright leaves.

Grasmere woodland scene

In the atmospheric woodland between Grasmere and Rydal Water you do not need strong sunlight to be able to appreciate the glory of autumn. On this day there was only the gentlest of winds and this allowed the trees and grasses in their golden colours to shimmer in the waters of the lake.

Footbridge in the woodland

There are pictures to be found in every corner of a wood like this. Here, the little footbridge gives a focus to this typical woodland scene.

97

White Moss towards Easdale

The little fell of White Moss is situated between Grasmere and Rydal Water. Its top is a miniature wilderness of trees scattered among rocky hummocks with patches of marshland between. Here we look across the marshy land and its sunlit grasses with the two silver birches framing the distant snow-capped fell top of Sergeant Man (2,394ft/730m). On the left Silver How is in shadow.

Grasmere from White Moss

Look over the rocky outcrop and you are presented with glorious views of Grasmere. This photograph shows the island in the middle of the lake, so often seen and photographed from the road, with a lovely mix of autumn colours and evergreen trees surrounding the little building in the middle. The trees on the slopes of White Moss add a natural frame to the picture.

Rydal Water from White Moss

Look over the opposite edge from White Moss and you will see panoramic views out across Rydal Water and the fells beyond. Loughrigg Fell, on the right, is seen here in the shadow of the early morning winter sun. The rest of the scene is in bright sunshine, from the foreground grasses to the distant, snow-covered Wansfell Pike.

White Moss trees

This photograph is taken at dawn on a wet and misty autumn day on the wooded path coming down from White Moss Fell. A sudden burst of sunshine lit up the view. There was no time to set up a tripod as light such as this is so transitory, but a photograph taken with a hand-held camera caught the moment perfectly.

View of the woods below White Moss

This colourful, early autumn scene, also taken in the White Moss woods below the fell, shows the trees in all their variety. Lying as they do between Grasmere and Rydal Water the woods are an excellent spot from which to explore the surrounding area and some of the best-loved spots in the Lake District.

Chapter 8
The central valleys

THE CENTRAL VALLEYS of the Lake District are located on either side of Grasmere and Rydal Water – and form the main north-south route through the Lakes. To the north is Thirlmere and the watershed of Dunmail Raise and to the south, Ambleside and Windermere. Kirkstone Pass, at 1,489ft (454m) is the highest road pass in the Lake District and guards the southern approach to the region. This is an area of high, desolate moorland with many fast-flowing streams and waterfalls. The long, thin lake of Thirlmere, which lies to the north, is one of the few lakes accessible by car or on foot.

Cold winter tree

In this photograph of the fellside in St John's in the Vale you can almost feel the cold of winter. St John's links Blencathra, one of the Lake District's most dramatic peaks, and Thirlmere via an impressively steep valley. This evocatively named area contains many remnants of the old quarrying industry.

St John's in the Vale with Blencathra

St John's in the Vale may have no lake to boast of but it does have an enthusiastic band of followers who love its rugged scenery. You only have to walk a short distance on to the fells, as seen here under the lea of Helvellyn, to experience glorious views. In the background Blencathra, with its familiar but dramatic skyline, sits astride the northern end of the vale with Rake Howe looming in the middle distance.

Thirlmere winter's day

Thirlmere is one of the Lake District's two main reservoirs – the other is Haweswater. Often the tidemark around this narrow lake left by lowering levels of water can spoil the view. On this crystal clear sunlit day, however, the reservoir was full. There had been a sharp air frost the night before and the fells behind were dusted with snow. The water near the edge of the lake was covered in the shoots of little trees coated in crystallised frost.

Light through frosted trees

The combination of bright sunshine and frost often produces some startling images. Here light shining through frosted trees and grasses gives them an almost luminous effect.

Frosted tree shoots in water

Little "ice trees" are formed in frosty weather and on a still day they are often perfectly reflected in the tranquil waters of the lake. When this photograph was taken there were so many of them that it was difficult to isolate a particular group.

West from Kirkstone Pass

This photograph (right) is taken from the top of "The Struggle", the long climb up from Ambleside towards the Kirkstone Pass. In the glow of late afternoon there is just enough light to illuminate the snow on the fellsides and the wet road but down below Windermere and Blelham Tarn are clearly visible. Look into the far distance and there, on the edge of the horizon, the sea is glinting in the light of early evening.

Stock Ghyll waterfall

Stock Ghyll Force, a dramatic waterfall on a tributary of the River Rothay, is a short walk from the centre of Ambleside. In the past, Stock Ghyll powered a number of watermills to fuel local industry. Photographically, waterfalls can often look at their best on a dull day. Using a slow shutter speed, coupled with a tripod, the waters of Stock Ghyll jump out from their cluttered surroundings, and there is a real sensation of movement as water crashes down the falls.

Sunset at Waterhead

In winter, it is worth looking towards the far south-west to have any chance of catching a dramatic sunset. This photograph was taken on a January day, as the sky was reddening over Waterhead on Windermere. Here the sun dips down below the fells, as its final rays illuminate the yachts swinging gently at anchor.

Chapter 9
Brothers Water to Haweswater

CONTINUE OVER the Kirkstone Pass and down the other side and you will soon come to the little glacial lake of Brothers Water as it nestles into Patterdale. This is another of those small peaceful locations where the lake can, occasionally, remain tranquil for much of the day. You can either take a gentle stroll around the lake, or be more energetic and climb up into the surrounding fells. Alternatively, you could walk from the little village of Hartsop near the foot of the lake, up onto the Knott and Angle Crags, to view the mountain tarns and reservoirs. Or, if you continue over the fell via the route of the Coast to Coast walk, you will experience the dramatic surroundings of the Haweswater reservoir.

Winter light on the reeds

One can never fail to be attracted to the splendid bank of reeds that surrounds the head of Brothers Water, especially when the light shines on them. The light was exceptionally good on the New Year's Eve when this photograph was taken, providing a contrast between the almost luminous, sunlit rushes and the more subdued bluish-white of the snow-clad fell behind. A lonely waterfowl ploughs its solitary way through the icy water.

Brothers Water from the outflow

Brothers Water, a quiet glacial lake, lies in Patterdale at the foot of Kirkstone Pass. This little lake is sheltered from the wind and its peaceful location gives rise to superb reflections that can remain all day. This photograph was taken on an early spring morning. The combination of a shimmering reflection combined with the light and shadow caused by the clouds passing overhead accentuates the beauty of this lake which is surrounded by the high fells.

View towards Dovedale (right)

A September walk along the eastern shore of Brothers Water brings this colourful shot across the lake towards Dovedale. There is just a hint of the forthcoming autumn colour which is enhanced by the water lily leaves to the bottom right. The little white puffy cloud in an otherwise clear blue sky adds an interesting touch.

View across to Hartsop

As you walk along the track that skirts the western side of Brothers Water your view of the lake is constantly interrupted by the trees that grow down to the water's edge. This photograph is taken across the lake towards the village of Hartsop with Brock Crags towering behind. It almost conveys the feeling that you are peering through the trees to the village in the distance.

Sheep reflections

This tranquil scene of sheep on the shoreline at Brothers Water was almost taken by chance. The sheep were suddenly spotted at the water's edge, beautifully grouped at the edge of the lake. The clear reflections, even at midday, coupled with the effect of the backlighting on the reeds, helped to create this picture.

Angle Tarn above Patterdale

Climb out of Patterdale and onto the fells to the east and you will soon come to the lovely spread of water which is Angle Tarn. Set in a shallow bowl of land high above Patterdale the random shape of the tarn only serves to enhance its beauty. There is always an air of peace and tranquillity here which is captured in this view across the tarn towards Brock Crags, which overlook the valley below in the distance.

Hayswater and High Street from Satura Crag

Carry on past Angle Tarn and you will shortly find yourself on Satura Crag, a rocky outcrop which overlooks Hayswater. This little pool of water, among the rocks on Satura Crag, is only a few feet across but makes a fine foreground to this photograph. This panoramic scene, with its spectacular sky, shows Hayswater with High Street Fell in the distance. High Street is part of the route of an old Roman road and horse races used to be held each year on its summit.

Winter view toward Kidsty Howe

Haweswater is another of the Lake District's reservoirs, and is set among glorious scenery. Riggindale can be seen in the far distance on the left, with the fell of Kidsty Howe to its right, where Wainwright's Coast to Coast walk starts its descent out of the Lakeland fells. There are no true reflections on this day but there is still a sheen on the otherwise blue water caused by the light from the snow-clad fells catching on the surface of the reservoir.

Haweswater and the far fells

This is a panoramic view across Haweswater on a fine February day. The impressive line of snow-covered hills at the far side shows Illgill (1,998ft/609m), on the left, Eagle Crag (1,709ft/521m) in the centre and High Street (2,717ft/828m) at the back and to the right.

Mardale in changeable weather

Further up Haweswater is Mardale. This village was submerged when the Haweswater valley was flooded in 1935 to provide water for the city of Manchester. In this photograph you can clearly see the scarred waterline of the reservoir.

Riggindale and the reservoir

Water levels can significantly change the appearance of a reservoir such as Haweswater. This photograph was taken on a day of changeable weather in autumn when the water level was low after a period of dry weather. The islands have enlarged and merged into one and, on the far side, where Riggindale meets the reservoir, field patterns from the past, normally submerged, have been exposed to view.

Chapter 10

Ullswater

THE FINAL part of our journey takes us down Patterdale from Brothers Water to Ullswater, the second largest lake in the Lake District. There is a timeless quality to Ullswater that has never been spoiled by commercialism or tourists. In the summer, the lake is dotted with the colourful sails of yachts and steamers cruise its length. Yet it is one of those places that always feels intimate despite its size. From Pooley Bridge, the lake stretches in a south-westerly direction for about eight miles. Around almost every corner are little gems to be explored and enjoyed. It is a place to linger and return to often; in spring and summer, when the sunrises can be spectacular, and into the autumn, when the colours of the beeches along the lakesides are second to none, to winter when the light is at its very best.

Ullswater sunrise

In summer the sunrises over Ullswater can be spectacular. This photograph was taken just after 5.30am in August, when the sun was rising in a clear eastern sky and the light was bouncing off the cloud cover over the lake. The result was this dramatic and colourful scene – just one of a number of varied shots taken during a glorious hour or so that day.

Ullswater morning – the boathouse

As you approach Ullswater from the direction of the main A66 this is the very first view that you get of a lake in the Lake District. If you can catch it in conditions such as these it is without doubt one of the most stunning views that you will see in the whole of this area of outstanding natural beauty. This photograph was taken shortly after sunrise with the mist clearing from the lake and the sun lighting up the old boathouse. Five minutes later the mists had cleared and the reflection was lost, but the magic of those few minutes will remain forever.

Place Fell from Glenridding

In the sheltered area of water near the head of Ullswater, at
Glenridding, the reflections can remain well into the day. This
photograph was taken at approximately 11am when all the conditions
seemed right. Late November snows dust Place Fell, so that the
autumn colours are mixed with a touch of winter. The still waters of
Ullswater with their almost perfect reflection complete the scene.

Pooley Bridge ferry terminal (right)

There is almost an ethereal feel to this photograph of Ullswater which
is created by the sunlight shining off the surface of the lake. It was a
cool January day with a lazy wind, just enough to lift the flag at the
end of the jetty. The angle at which the photograph was taken has
produced what is virtually a monochromatic image. The distant
shadowy shapes of Hallin Fell in front and Place Fell just behind add
to the mood of this picture.

Sheffield Pike

In winter, with the sun rising in the south-east, the early morning rays light up the fells surrounding Sheffield Pike (2,232ft/680m) and leave the lower levels in a cool shadow. The drama of the resulting scene is clear. The warmth of the light just after sunrise turns the snow-covered fell tops a glorious mixture of colours, which is then reflected in the still waters of the lake below.

Glencoyne Wood beech tree

The trees along the sides of Ullswater are renowned for the glorious colours they display in autumn. This is especially true of some of the majestic beech trees that grow near the side of the lake in Glencoyne Wood. This stunning example is one of many where the sun, having risen over Place Fell, now pours its light across the lake and through the branches and leaves, creating a kaleidoscope of colour which contrasts with the silhouette of the tree trunk.

Tree framing golden bracken

It is not only trees which provide autumn colour – the golden-coloured bracken below the trees can also add to the glory that is autumn in Ullswater. In this photograph, framed by a craggy old oak tree, we look through to the glorious golden colours beyond. In Glencoyne Wood there is a network of paths which allow you to enjoy these autumnal scenes yet still have excellent views over Ullswater.

Landscape in miniature

This little scene captures the essence of an autumn woodland. The orangey-red grasses are balanced by the colours of the leaves, ranging from yellow and green through to brown, with the shiny tree trunk providing a stark contrast.

Glenridding misty morning

The photograph on the left was taken by the side of Ullswater on what promised to be a fine day with light mist and cloud drifting across the scene. As the winter sun rises above Place Fell on the left it sent a brilliant quality of light across the lake. With the stillness of the water and the mirror-like reflection the scene has an almost ethereal quality. Within minutes a great swathe of mist descended on Ullswater. The photograph above shows how rapidly the whole of the lake was completely shrouded in mist, almost blotting out the sun completely.

Gowbarrow dawn light

This view looks across Ullswater in the light of dawn near Gowbarrow – the spot which inspired the Lake District's most famous son, the Romantic poet William Wordsworth, to write his best-loved poem on the subject of daffodils. This photograph catches the reflected light of a winter sunrise and, with its rose-tinted hues, brilliantly reflects the glory of dawn in the lakes.

Evening peace – from Pooley Bridge

We finish with a shot taken after the sun has set on a beautifully still Ullswater. As we look
up the lake from near Pooley Bridge to the fells in the distance, the softly-muted hues of
the afterglow of sunset create a scene that is a haven of peace and tranquillity.
It is a view where, perhaps, you can dwell awhile in its mood of quietness and let your
mind run back over memories of this beautiful landscape.